DATE DUE

W9-ABU-138

Put Beginning Readers on the Right Track with
ALL ABOARD READING™

The All Aboard Reading series is especially designed for beginning readers. Written by noted authors and illustrated in full color, these are books that children really want to read—books to excite their imagination, expand their interests, make them laugh, and support their feelings. With fiction and nonfiction stories that are high interest and curriculum-related, All Aboard Reading books offer something for every young reader. And with four different reading levels, the All Aboard Reading series lets you choose which books are most appropriate for your children and their growing abilities.

Picture Readers

Picture Readers have super-simple texts, with many nouns appearing as rebus pictures. At the end of each book are 24 flash cards—on one side is a rebus picture; on the other side is the written-out word.

Station Stop 1

Station Stop 1 books are best for children who have just begun to read. Simple words and big type make these early reading experiences more comfortable. Picture clues help children to figure out the words on the page. Lots of repetition throughout the text helps children to predict the next word or phrase—an essential step in developing word recognition.

Station Stop 2

Station Stop 2 books are written specifically for children who are reading with help. Short sentences make it easier for early readers to understand what they are reading. Simple plots and simple dialogue help children with reading comprehension.

Station Stop 3

Station Stop 3 books are perfect for children who are reading alone. With longer text and harder words, these books appeal to children who have mastered basic reading skills. More complex stories captivate children who are ready for more challenging books.

In addition to All Aboard Reading books, look for All Aboard Math Readers™ (fiction stories that teach math concepts children are learning in school); All Aboard Science Readers™ (nonfiction books that explore the most fascinating science topics in age-appropriate language); All Aboard Poetry Readers™ (funny, rhyming poems for readers of all levels); and All Aboard Mystery Readers™ (puzzling tales where children piece together evidence with the characters).

All Aboard for happy reading!

To my grandmothers Wanda Laird Wilkinson
and Anne Hamilton and grandmothers-in-
law Josephine Clarke and Vera Williams, for
showing me love and teaching me graciousness,
fortitude, and adaptability—G.L.C.

To my wife, Dorothy, and daughter, Nyanza—
M.R.

GROSSET & DUNLAP
Published by the Penguin Group
Penguin Group (USA) Inc., 375 Hudson Street, New York, New York 10014, U.S.A.
Penguin Group (Canada), 10 Alcorn Avenue, Toronto, Ontario, Canada M4V 3B2
(a division of Pearson Penguin Canada Inc.)
Penguin Books Ltd, 80 Strand, London WC2R 0RL, England
Penguin Ireland, 25 St Stephen's Green, Dublin 2, Ireland
(a division of Penguin Books Ltd)
Penguin Group (Australia), 250 Camberwell Road, Camberwell, Victoria 3124, Australia
(a division of Pearson Australia Group Pty Ltd)
Penguin Books India Pvt Ltd, 11 Community Centre,
Panchsheel Park, New Delhi - 110 017, India
Penguin Group (NZ), Cnr Airborne and Rosedale Roads, Albany, Auckland 1310, New Zealand
(a division of Pearson New Zealand Ltd)
Penguin Books (South Africa) (Pty) Ltd, 24 Sturdee Avenue,
Rosebank, Johannesburg 2196, South Africa

Penguin Books Ltd, Registered Offices:
80 Strand, London WC2R 0RL, England

Library of Congress Control Number: 2004017866

ISBN 0-448-43120-3 (pbk)   10 9 8 7 6 5 4 3 2

ISBN 0-448-43828-3 (hc)   10 9 8 7 6 5 4 3 2 1

GiaNt LizarDs

By Ginjer L. Clarke
Illustrated by Michael Rothman

Grosset & Dunlap

Lizards come in many sizes.
Some are small
and make good pets.
But other lizards are huge
and ferocious.

Here are some of the

biggest, fiercest reptiles

from all over the world.

This huge lizard flicks its yellow,

forked tongue in and out.

It smells the air

for dead meat to eat.

It has terrible breath.

Its teeth are as sharp as needles,

its claws are like razors,

and it is covered with rough scales.

Is it a fire-breathing dragon? Almost.

It is a Komodo dragon!

Komodo dragons (say: cuh-MOE-do)
live on Komodo Island
and a few other small islands
in the Pacific Ocean.
The numbers of dragons and people
on these islands are almost equal.

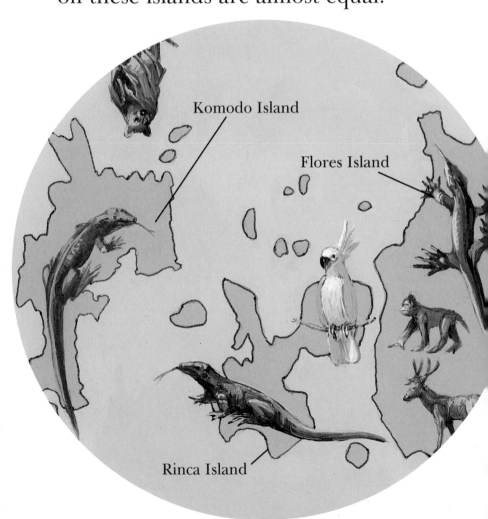

Komodo Island

Flores Island

Rinca Island

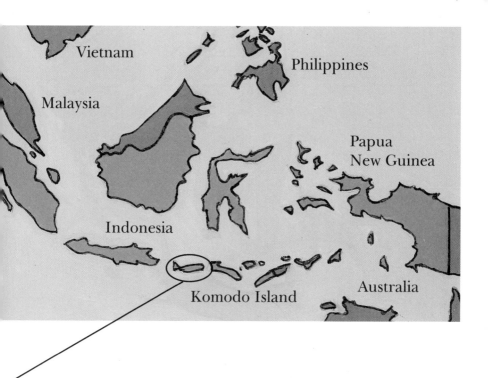

The people on these islands

stay away from the dragons

most of the time.

The dragons could hurt the people

if they get too close.

Komodo dragons have even

killed a few people!

The Komodo dragon
is the largest monitor lizard.
There are about 30 types
of monitor lizards.

You can identify a monitor lizard by
its forked tongue and large, strong tail.
The Komodo dragon can be ten feet long.
That's longer than a car!
It can weigh more than 300 pounds—
the same as you and five friends.

These Komodo dragons
are eating their dinner.
The dragons can swallow
huge bites of food.
They open their mouths very wide
just like a snake.
Komodo dragons eat deer, birds, goats,
and water buffalo.

But the dragons mostly like to eat

animals that are already dead.

That is why the dragons

have such bad breath—phew!

Komodo dragons move very fast

when they hunt.

They can climb trees.

And they are good swimmers.

But they are usually lazy.

After eating, they lie around

in the sun and drool—

what bad manners!

The Galápagos Islands

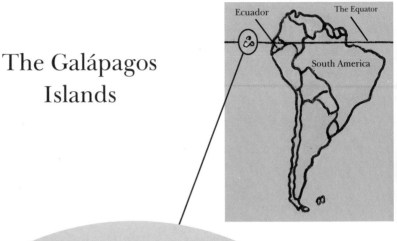

Like Komodo dragons,

marine iguanas (say: igg-WAN-ah)

also live on islands

in the Pacific Ocean.

These huge lizards sit
in large groups on the jagged rocks.
Marine iguanas soak up the sun
to keep warm.

Marine iguanas are

the only lizards that

live part of their lives

in the ocean.

The word "marine" means "of the sea."

Marine iguanas use their tails like oars.

The lizards slide through

the water like snakes.

After the sun sets

and the tide goes out,

marine iguanas dive

into the cold water

to look for algae to eat.

With their strong jaws,

they twist and pull

the algae off the rocks.

Algae is the only food they eat.

On these same islands,
land iguanas live
with the marine iguanas.
But the land iguanas
do not swim.
And they eat cacti
instead of algae.

23

Land iguanas are much fiercer
than their marine cousins.
And they like to be alone
instead of in groups.

They will fight each other

until one of them

bleeds and gives up.

In the treetops of a
South American rain forest,
another kind of iguana sits
on a small branch.
The green iguana holds onto the
branch using its curved claws.

Its extra-long tail helps it balance.

Green iguanas eat mostly leaves,

berries, and fruit that they

find in the treetops.

On the ground below the trees,

this female green iguana

is laying her eggs.

She can lay up to 60 eggs at one time.

She buries her eggs safely

in a tunnel in the sand.

About three months later,

the bright green baby lizards

hatch all at once.

Green iguanas are often
sold in pet stores.
People like their long tails,
bright colors, spiny backs,
and floppy throat flaps.
But green iguanas can be mean.

They whip their tails and
fight with their sharp claws.
They are not friendly pets.

In the Arizona desert is another
lizard that would not
make a good pet.
It is the Gila monster (say: HEE-lah).
Even its name sounds scary!

It has bumpy skin like a basketball.

Like the Komodo dragon,

it has a forked tongue.

But worst of all,

the Gila monster is poisonous!

It kills animals by biting them

and sending venom

from its teeth.

It eats rats, birds' eggs,

rabbits, and smaller lizards.

Another giant lizard,

the Nile monitor,

lives far away in Africa.

Its name comes from

the Nile River in Egypt.

This giant lizard sits on a rock

along the riverbank.

Crocodiles also live here.

When a crocodile attacks a Nile monitor,
the lizard dives into the water
and swims away to safety.
It uses its strong, flat tail
to move quickly.

This Nile monitor

rears up on its hind legs

to scare away another lizard.

It puffs out its neck sac

and hisses loudly.

S-S-s-s!

When two Nile monitors wrestle,

they look like they are dancing.

This dancing fight is finished

when one lizard pushes

the other lizard over.

This female
Nile monitor
is laying her eggs.
She does not make a nest.
Instead, she rips open
the wall of a termite mound.
She lays up to 30 eggs
at the end of a long tunnel.

When the termites fix the nest,

they seal the lizard eggs inside.

When the baby lizards hatch,

they eat the termites.

The perentie lizard (say: puh-REN-tee)

lives in the Australian desert.

Its polka dots

help it hide in the sand.

The perentie can run a short distance
upright on its hind legs.
Its tail is so strong that
it can knock a person down—
or break a dog's leg.

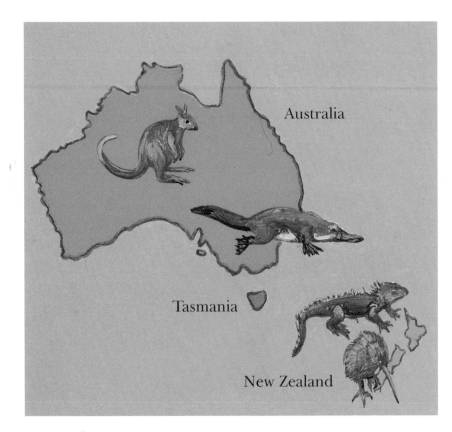

The tuatara (say: too-ah-TAR-ah)

lives only on New Zealand.

The tuatara looks like a lizard, but it is not.

The tuatara is a reptile,

but it is in a group by itself.

Its bones and teeth are different

from those of the lizards.

The oddest thing about the tuatara

is its third eye.

This eye cannot see.

It is covered with skin and can sense light.

Some scientists think that the tuatara

probably used this extra eye

a long time ago.

Sphenodon-Tuatara

pineal gland

The pineal
gland=
"the third eye"

The tuatara has been around
since the time of the dinosaurs.
Scientists call it a "living fossil."
The word "dinosaur" means
"terrible lizard."

All of the tuatara's other
relatives are now extinct.
That means they are all gone.

These days, the dinosaurs are all gone.

And dragons are not real.

But giant lizards

are here to stay!